# SAGEBRUSH VERNACULAR
## Rural Architecture in Nevada

*Happy Birthday 2003*

Edited by Stephen R. Davis

Photographs by Peter Goin's Advanced Photography Class at the University of Nevada, Reno

Essays contributed by Jill Derby, Peter Goin, Linda Hussa, Paul Oatman, and Paul Starrs

Nevada Humanities Committee
**2003**

D1706838

Funded by grants from the E. L. Cord Foundation and the Clark J. Guild Jr. Charitable Foundation.
Photographs made possible by a grant from the E. L. Wiegand Foundation.

# Sagebrush Vernacular: Rural Architecture in Nevada

© Copyright Nevada Humanities Committee, 2003
Based on the Nevada Humanities Committee's exhibit *Sagebrush Vernacular: Rural Architecture in Nevada. Sagebrush Vernacular* accompanied the Smithsonian Institution's *Barn Again!*® exhibit tour of Nevada in 2003.

A Halcyon Imprint of the
Nevada Humanities Committee
1034 North Sierra Street, Reno, Nevada 89507
ISBN 1-890591-14-9
Designed by Nancy Peppin
Cover photograph: David W. Colborn. General view, Willow Creek Ranch. See page 74

*The Nevada Humanities Committee logo is derived from a petroglyph representing a human hand located at Rattlesnake Well, Mineral County, Nevada, ca. 800 – 1200 A.D.*

**Nevada Humanities Committee**
The Nevada Humanities Committee was established in 1971 to enrich the lives of all Nevadans through the humanities. Funded in part by the National Endowment for the Humanities, the Nevada Humanities Committee is an independent, non-profit organization. The Humanities Committee works in partnership with local communities to develop and fund humanities programs for diverse audiences—programs that encourage the discovery of the humanities in interesting and thought-provoking ways.

Ikue Yada. Trimmer Barn, Genoa.

# Acknowledgments

Several generous donors made this book possible. The E. L. Cord Foundation and the Clark J. Guild Jr. Charitable Foundation made significant contributions to the production of the *Sagebrush Vernacular* book. The E. L. Wiegand Foundation provided major funding to bring the *Barn Again!*® and *Sagebrush Vernacular* programs to the people of Nevada.

Professor Peter Goin of the University of Nevada, Reno, Art Department, played an important role throughout the project. He helped develop the concept of *Sagebrush Vernacular*, oversaw the production of the photographs, and contributed an article to this publication.

Deborah J. Cruze provided invaluable assistance in the preparation of the photographic archive, in curating the exhibit, and in taking supplemental photographs to complete the exhibit.

We are also indebted to the staff of the Nevada State Historic Preservation Office, particularly Ronald M. James, State Historic Preservation Officer and Historian; Mella Rothwell Harmon, Historic Preservation Specialist; and researcher Elizabeth Safford Harvey.

Professor James W. Hulse, Emeritus Professor of History at the University of Nevada, Reno, read portions of the text for accuracy.

A number of barn experts and preservationists have assisted in the preparation of this book including Paul Oatman, Jack P. Hursh, Jr., and Loren Jahn.

Local sponsors and coordinators hosted the two exhibits and developed numerous public programs in their communities. These are Tamara Woods and Beezy Tobiasson of the Old Logandale School Historical and Cultural Society, Jesse Davis and Greg Seymour of Las Vegas Springs Preserve, Jane Pieplow of Churchill County Museum, Jeff Glavor of Bartley Ranch Regional Park in Reno, Mary Ellen Conaway of Carson Valley Museum and Cultural Center, and Meg Glaser of Western Folklife Center in Elko.

The Museum on Main Street staff, Carol Harsh, Brian Crockett, Rozanna Sokolowski, and Esther MacIntosh, gave support throughout this project.

Thanks to our contributing authors Jill Derby, Peter Goin, Linda Hussa, Paul Oatman, and Paul Starrs.

Finally, we want to recognize the photographers who contributed to this volume: Catana L. Barnes, Thomas Sanford Drew Boyer, David W. Colborn, Deborah J. Cruze, Laura Fillmore, Micah Silva-Frank, Meranda Gerlock, Dustin Ray Hartman, LaMont Johnson, Aimee Lopes, Amber Lee Martin, Andrea Martinez, Jennifer Ober, R. Nelson Parrish, Nick Profaizer, Ryan Quinlan, Ariana Page Russell, Arlo Schenk, Anna Schooley, Jessica Slack, Tsunaki Tabayashi, Matt Theilen, David Brendan Torch, and Ikue Yada.

# Contributors

## Jill Derby

Jill Talbot Derby earned her Ph.D. in Anthropology from the University of California, Davis in 1988, the same year she was elected to the Board of Regents of the University and Community College System of Nevada. Her dissertation was entitled *Cattle, Kin and the Patrimonial Imperative: Social Organization on Nevada Family Ranches*.

## Peter Goin

Peter Goin is a Professor of Art in photography and video at the University of Nevada, Reno. He is the author of numerous books and articles including *A Doubtful River, Nuclear Landscapes* and *Stopping Time: A Rephotographic Survey of Lake Tahoe*. His photographs have been exhibited in more than fifty museums nationally and internationally, and he is the recipient of two National Endowment for the Arts Fellowships.

## Linda Hussa

Linda Hussa is a poet and rancher who lives in Surprise Valley, near the small town of Cedarville in northeastern California. She has published books of poetry, short stories, articles, and essays. These include *Lige Langston: Sweet Iron*, a lyrical biography of a Nevada buckaroo, and *Blood Sister, I Am To These Fields*.

## Paul Oatman

Paul Oatman is a writer, photographer, and timber framer. His pen and camera have recorded timber frame structures as far east as Poland. He stumbled on the barns of Carson Valley seven years ago and has been surveying them ever since. He lives in Pioneer, California.

## Paul Starrs

Professor Paul Starrs teaches cultural and historical geography at the University of Nevada, Reno, where he works on a variety of topics associated with the landscape history and geography of the "New West." He is the author of *Let the Cowboy Ride: Cattle Ranching in the American West*.

## Stephen Davis

Stephen Davis is the Assistant Director of the Nevada Humanities Committee and the statewide coordinator for the *Barn Again!*® tour of Nevada. He earned his Ph.D. in early American history from the University of Wisconsin, Madison, and is also a documentary photographer who has taught photography at the university level.

Deborah J. Cruze. Bunkhouse, Recanzone Ranch, Paradise Valley.

# Contents

# Foreword *Jill Derby*

Stories of urban flight abound. We read of Americans fleeing the congestion and stress of city living in search of a simpler life in small towns and rural spaces. Émigrés from urban America are pursuing visions of a tranquil and unspoiled life built on images of an earlier time when small town life was mainstream and rural landscapes prominent. As cities expanded and towns grew to become cities and suburbs, those rural landscapes faded from our national focus. Television directed our attention to urban spaces and international scenes. Yet certain images remain in our social memory as reminders of another way of life, a time when the rhythm of life was drawn from the cycles of nature and the primary need for sustenance. Barns are one of those reminder images the nation holds.

Barns in popular culture have come to represent more than just a place to store hay, tractors, and saddles. Barns and saddles, boots and spurs are physical expressions of livelihood on the one hand, yet sources of cultural fascination on the other. The answer to the question of why these rural, agrarian symbols have acquired romantic and nostalgic meaning is deeply embedded in the national memory of westward expansion and conquering the frontier. The themes of adventure, freedom, and the conquest of nature all intertwine around these symbols, and their evolution into popular icons reveals how rapid and profound change leaves us longing for what is left behind.

A study of western Nevada cattle ranching families is illustrative of the pressures and trends felt widely by family owned and operated ranches in many parts of the West. In the irrigated valleys of western Nevada where the eastern slopes of the Sierra Nevada Mountains meet the western edge of the Great Basin, ranch land has dwindled because of the steady population growth that the attractions of the region inspire. Émigrés from California's sprawling cities bolting from the congestion, pollution, and aggravations of urban life have driven land values up dramatically in their quest for clean air, mountain scenery, and recreational opportunities. As a result of this increased value of land in my home area of Carson Valley, many ranchers who live frugally on modest incomes have become paper millionaires.

More typically for family ranchers, raising cattle is a modestly profitable enterprise. Factors such as market volatility, production costs, weather vagaries, and disease contribute to the uncertainty of beef production. Ranchers never know from year to year what their income will be. Two mitigating factors which allow ranchers to stay in business in the least profitable times are the lack of debt on ranch holdings, which most often have been passed down in the families for some generations, and the use of family and volunteer labor for ranch work.

While increased land value would seem a favorable development for those owning land, ranchers committed to staying in business and passing the ranch on from father to son do not benefit. Having a large ranch holding is a requirement for ranching, yet operating as they do on modest profit margins, ranchers cannot afford to buy more land to enhance their operations. Most ranches in western Nevada can run at best only one cow-calf unit per acre, and in other parts of Nevada that ratio is much higher. It is not economical to pay high prices for land, given that kind of utilization limitation. More seriously, high land values jeopardize the possibility of passing on the ranch to the next generation. High inheritance taxes are likely to force heirs to sell land to pay the debt. Thus, while the escalation of land values increases a rancher's equity, it also increases the pressure to succumb to suburban development and abandon ranching.

Another factor working against ranch sustainability is the tension and conflict that accompany suburban development in formerly agricultural communities. Of particular frustration to ranchers is the increased competition they experience for public land use with the growing numbers of recreation seekers. Traditionally, ranchers have had exclusive use of these lands for grazing livestock—an important part of the economic equation in ranching. Growing populations bring others into the picture, such as hikers, bikers, hunters, fishermen, and off road vehicle enthusiasts. The federal agencies which manage these lands must try to balance access to the land among these competing interest groups.

A second source of tension revolves around issues of compatibility. While most people move from cities to the countryside for the bucolic ambience, there are aggravations in rural settings as well. Most secondary roads are two-lane; when the reality sets in of waiting fifteen minutes on thc way to an appointment for a cattle herd to switch pastures, tempers flare. New residents may decide that they prefer the pastures to the cattle and tractors that go with them. The policies of local governments soon begin to reflect the shift in demographics. Perhaps the images and symbols of our rural heritage are dearer to us than the real thing.

Whatever the fate of the ranches and farms in our countryside today, they remain a proud part of our national heritage and a bulwark of meaning to our sense of historical identity. Barns conjure up a longing for a simpler era when life was uncomplicated. The symbols of cattle ranching—boots, spurs, branding irons, saddles, lariats, and Stetsons—evoke a different response. They reflect an image of a rugged, independent life in the out of doors, a life of self-sufficiency, physical challenge, and freedom. Idealized as ranching has been in the popular mind, there is an aura surrounding it that conveys a set of values—freedom, courage, independence, and toughness.

Symbols play a powerful role in human communication. They often embody and convey more meaning than those who adopt and claim them can articulate. Symbols such as barns, boots, and branding irons are distinctly American and call forth the pride and attachment Americans share in their rural and pioneer beginnings.

# Introduction    *Stephen R. Davis*

*Sagebrush Vernacular: Rural Architecture in Nevada* documents Nevada's ranching and agricultural heritage. Nevada Humanities Committee created the *Sagebrush Vernacular* exhibit and this book to preserve this aspect of Nevada's rural history and to bring it to the people of the state.

Sagebrush Vernacular* complements the Smithsonian Institution's traveling exhibit *Barn Again: Celebrating an American Icon.* Nevada Humanities Committee brought both exhibits to seven Nevada communities in 2003. *Barn Again!*® offers an overview of the American barn from its European roots, through its varying roles in different regions of the United States, to its iconic function in American popular culture. Given these many goals, it can only tangentially touch on vernacular architecture in the West. Nevada Humanities Committee believes that *Sagebrush Vernacular*, which concentrates on Nevada rural architecture, provides a valuable local context through which to understand *Barn Again!*® The Museum on Main Street program made *Barn Again!*® available to the Nevada Humanities Committee, the state affiliate of the National Endowment for the Humanities. (MOMS is a collaboration between the Smithsonian Institution Traveling Exhibition Service and the Federation of State Humanities Councils.)

Much research still needs to be done on Nevada's rural architecture or, indeed, on life in rural Nevada. While large agricultural states, such as those in the Midwest, have a long tradition of scholarship regarding their agricultural history,

architecture, and sociology, not enough has been done in Nevada. It is true that a number of scholars and institutions have contributed to our understanding of Nevada's rural architecture, including the Nevada State Historic Preservation Office, the late Blanton Owen, and Thomas Carter of the University of Utah. Still, we can point to only a limited number of articles, a few books, some unpublished research, and a major Library of Congress study from the early 1980s entitled *Buckaroos in Paradise*, which focuses on folklife in Paradise Valley, Nevada. We hope that *Sagebrush Vernacular* will raise public interest in Nevada's rural architectural heritage and encourage further scholarly activity.

Nevada agriculture is largely hidden. Travelers on interstate highways see few signs that ranching and agriculture play an economic and cultural role in the state. Yet a mixed agriculture and ranching economy sprang up in Nevada at the time of the earliest settlements. During the state's early history, as mining districts convulsed through the boom and bust cycle, it was the state's agricultural and ranching communities, such as Yerington, Panaca, Elko, and Fallon, that provided stability and leadership for Nevada.

Nevada's well-watered valleys are scattered, but where they exist they provide a paradise for all forms of life from antelope to cattle. On the other hand, even in these comparatively fertile environments resources are limited. Particularly for the earliest settlers, who relied solely on indigenous resources, building in Nevada posed a particular challenge. Settlements near the highest mountains, such as Carson Valley near the Sierra Nevada, could build with tall, straight timbers. In these areas traditional timber-frame construction flourished.

Other communities had to rely on the limited materials at hand, such as stone and adobe for buildings and saplings and willows for fences and corrals. For example, in Paradise Valley, where stone and stonemasons from the Italian Piedmont came together, stone construction thrived.

As with all rural peoples, Nevada farmers and ranchers took advantage of every opportunity to utilize available materials. For instance, railroad tie structures proliferated as railroads either upgraded poor quality sections built in haste, replaced worn rights-of-way, or abandoned infrequently used routes. Ranchers and farmers built many structures, such as cabins, bunkhouses, and root cellars from railroad ties. In some cases they combined railroad ties with other materials such as timber and stone.

The photographs in the exhibit and in this book were taken in the fall of 2001 by a group of advanced photography students studying with Professor Peter Goin at the University of Nevada, Reno. After receiving an introduction to the project and some training in historical architecture and barn construction, students proceeded to divide themselves into groups which fanned out across the state. The results of their work are impressive. The photographic archive, resulting from this work has been deposited in Special Collections at the University of Nevada, Reno library.

Students approached their photographs differently. They traveled to different parts of the state, were drawn to different sorts of structures, and they brought widely divergent sensibilities to their subject. There were those who photographed in a straightforward yet subtle documentary style while others chose to use devices such as tilted frames or wide-angle lenses to communicate their reactions to their subjects. Some were drawn to dark barn interiors, others to the vast landscape of Nevada ranches, and still others to the details of construction such as timber-frame joinery. Although early in their careers, these student photographers have made a permanent contribution to our knowledge of life in rural Nevada.

Essays in this book contribute to our understanding of the *Sagebrush Vernacular* photographs and provide insight into life in the rural West.

Jill Derby's Foreword places the Nevada barn and other icons of ranch life in the context of the rapid social change overtaking the state. An anthropologist, Derby also comments on the paradox of the increasing loss of family ranches and the simultaneous conversion of everyday ranch objects, such as chaps, boots, and barns into icons of the American experience.

Professor Peter Goin, who helped design the *Sagebrush Vernacular* project and who supervised the taking of the photographs, describes the history of the project and provides insight into its significance.

Paul Oatman, a student and artisan of timber-frame buildings, provides insight into the history and construction of timber-frame barns in Europe and America. He also introduces us to Carson Valley's little known yet notable timber-frame barns.

Poet, essayist, and rancher Linda Hussa has contributed a piece of literary nonfiction entitled *In The Clearing*. Her spare yet lyrical essay ponders the origins of an abandoned barn in her neighborhood and the role that barns and barn building have played in her family.

Professor Paul Starrs, who has studied cowboys and ranching from the saddle and from behind his computer, considers the geographical context of the barn and its setting, the barnyard. Although both spaces have much in common, the barnyard provides a true blank slate for the evolving life of the ranch. It offers an organizing principle, a workspace, and a flexible environment for the economic, social, and material life of the ranch to occur.

# In The Clearing  *Linda Hussa*

The barn lived alone on the land, having passed beyond need. There on that low knoll, ground sloping away toward water in a shallow creek, trees well back, grass trod out for more than a century, the barn was at rest. I admired its correctness, its manner of belonging, its beauty beyond requirement, and knowing the affairs of barns, I admired the mind that built it, loving it, all of it in the course of daily toil. No fence tied to it, no posts set adjacent to control its line, no corrals holding it down, no other work connected it anymore, freed as a soul is freed from failing breath and string-halted stride. Yet it throbbed as light poured on it from a broken sky, deepening shadows, brightening cleanly each board from its companions, as a tree stands alone and also belongs to the forest in kinship, in wholeness, in desire. The sheer plane of the roof, the pitch to shed snow abruptly met the pace and rhythm of the walls' milled boards and bats. It was the flat of endless sky against mountain peaks; it was the horse's flat stride against once being wild; it was the flat gaze of the man set out to change the open country, to mark it by his very being, against his desire to let it remain so. I stopped at the roadside some distance away and stood at the fence, hands placed between barbs holding wire that still sang of cattle and horses and the dangers of living in a harsh land. Even from that distance I knew the boundless wish of the builder to make it sturdy and beautiful and true.

The barn grew from the ground, walls shoving upward from the loam as a tree parts the earth nudging aside red-top, or bluestem or timothy and opens the ground to the same sweet mullen or clover scent that drifts in the broad open meadow. The color of it belonged, blanched pine and iron warming under this light, gray as the grooves of other years in a man's eyes.

In the Great Basin, a barn roof is covered with cedar shingles or the rust and glinting of tin. Trees tight to the clearing's edge are piñon pine or juniper or mountain mahogany or cottonwood or willow. Sage and lupine and mule-ears dot rocky ground. Hawks, then. Wild geese. Curlews probing the marshes. Yellow headed blackbirds sorting cowpies for insects. Throughout the region the varieties of nature are controlled by water, and water is often scarce.

There is a haymow in the center of the barn. A long horse manger, saddle room, grain barrel on the lean-to side. Salt blocks stacked. Perhaps a stanchion, if there is a woman and children preferring fresh milk to canned and willing to take on the milking chores. Nearby, a calf pen, a milking stool and, hanging somewhere handy, a tub of bag balm. The barn, unlike the shop, or icehouse, or woodshed, implies community described by the evolution of caring between human and beast.

• • • • •

The earnest man, whose safety and work depends on horses in harness and under saddle, would not feed them moldy hay that would foul their lungs and cause them colic. Although cows grow fat on weedy hay that steams or smolders and stinks most

13

putrid, horses are sensitive to change in feed and intolerant of poorly cured hay. To keep his horses healthy and able to work he must build a barn to store their feed safe from spoilage and to protect harness, saddles, gear from sun and winter storms.

It was in light as clear as water this man walked the bare knoll. Wear streaked his dark trousers. The back and belly of his shirt billowed and snapped in the wind of evening's approach. His boots were high-heeled and lasted for riding, yet he strode out, hoping to prosper, to expand. Leaning down he knocked a peg into the ground, knotted a loop of string on it, and turned to measure out the dimension of the barn by his stride. Stick rattling in his hand. Twine running between his fingers, spinning like a bobbin as he walked, chin up, stepping to make a yard, counting as the shuffling string rubbed calluses from driving lines, calluses from the axe, calluses from the forge. At a number known only to him he stopped, rapped a second peg into the ground, double half-hitched the twine on the peg, cornered, walked again figuring in his head until he cornered again and again, until he met his beginning at the center door of the barn where the rail was to be hung and ropes would lift the fork and swing a great hunk of long hay into the mow. And now, hat brim blocking the sun, he scanned his land, imagining the view from the barn.

The plan began in solitary hours when he was half-asleep. It occupied him in the swirl of grounds in his coffee cup, or all the way home from town. In the dream he walked toward his barn on a snowy morning wrapped in a solitary sound. All else was obliterated by rank wind. He stepped inside and closed the door, yet the wind hung outside in the moaning, coaxing creak and lean of wood. In that half-light he knew the workhorses were turned to him with calm eyes. Their manure simply dropped where they stood tied would reassure him as clean and good. The geldings would know his form and voice and smell, nickering now, listening for the grainy sound of the scoop in the oat bin. Giving to his hand pressuring lightly on a hip to step aside, they would let him between bodies weighing near a ton with hooves the size of a supper plate. Huge heads and heavy manes pressed against his shoulders as he filled their feed boxes. He needed horses; could not tend the cattle without saddle horses; could not farm and feed without workhorses such as this team of Percherons. Nearly one horse in temperament, pulling even, working together, they were horses he could trust. At the gates he tied the lines on the Jacob staff, got off the wagon, opened the gate, clucked to them and they would walk through. When he said whoa, they would stop and stand, waiting for him to close the gate, get back on the wagon, and take up the lines. Quiet and easy all morning, pulling the wagon from field to field while he fed hay to the dry cows in the canyon, mother cows and calves in the rye field, weaners in the feedlot, bulls down in the lake field, and saddle horses in the willows. Thinking about all this he lingered in his dream, in the company of his horses chewing, releasing the starchy-sweet smell of oats.

(In the core
of each cell
patterned into man's being
does he recall
the path he walked
with all the beasts
of earth
and water
and sky ?

And then,
as intellect withered elsewhere
and bloomed in him
to stand upright
and speak,
was that why
he painted
horse
on cave walls ?

Was the promise
in the scripture of his species
to care for those
who did not rise
as he,
to revere his beginnings
recognizing

the wild inscription
in eyes
not unlike
his own ?

I must conclude
he could not go
alone.

Needing freedom
he chose horses
to lift him
and for that
he follows the commandment
made of light

to build a shelter,
harvest feed,
seek their company,
work beside them,
and weep
when they die.)

Brass buckles and studs ignited by sun. Dull black leather harness, supple with oil, hung from pegs on the upright logs that braced the outer wall. In his dream he brushed the horses, fit their collars, snug and padded, fastened at the neck, Brace first, then the young horse, Harry. At each gelding's shoulder and with momentum in his body and arms, he rocked and lifted the heavy, awkward harness in an arcing swing, tugs flung out long and trailing, settling the hames in the groove of the collar, the rest spread over the back and haunches. After buckling the belly-band where a saddlehorse's cinch would be, he stepped around to straighten the back straps and pull the britching down until it draped the horse like a net, to equalize the pull and stop. All the while he was touching, stroking, filling their waiting hearts with sounds that gave them ease. Their bodies, heavy with winter hair and thickened by half-days rest in winter, filled him in equal measure. Dependence held them together in part. Beyond, respect elevated them to friendship, just as his wife loved her cow and told her things only a woman would hear. Together they did the work of life. The horses pulled the implements to cultivate the land, harvest the wild hay, and then in the cycle of seasons, the wagon, as he forked hay to cows coming to the feed trail through the long months of winter. When the horses finished the oats he would untie their halter ropes and lead them to the door, well aware of their weight and size around him, alert to the possibilities of danger in their company. With his hat pulled down they would step into the storm.

At the wagon tongue with the mincing steps of a lady in a long skirt, they side-stepped into place. From in front of them, (this was the moment of greatest risk, before they were hooked solid to the wagon when a sudden noise might cause them to shy or pull away or knock him down) he reached down, jerked the tongue from the frozen ground, and snapped the neck yoke to their breast strap. Now, the wagon anchored the chance of fright, and his tension eased away. He took their bridles down, held the iron bits in his hands and warmed the steel with his breath before bridling them, tucking ears under, smoothing forelocks, buckling the throat latch, and the checks. Between their front legs the pole strap snapped into the neck yoke, then he hooked the tugs - outside first - to the double tree. Lines in hand he climbed up to stand behind the Jacob staff. Respectful of his horses, he never asked them to pull the wagon, empty or loaded, straight away from a dead stop, but stepped them to a slight angle and moved them off a rolling wheel on the quarter.

All this once he built the barn. Come spring, as soon as they could get into the mountains, they could begin. For now, he grained and harnessed the horses at the door of the shed in the open, hurrying, sour humor abiding, and the horses restless, wanting to turn tail to the storm. Cramped, shivering, his wife led the cow against the south side out of the wind, but not out of the cold. Hands reddened, fingers chapped. Cow's teats frostbit, bleeding. Milk freezing in the pail. And misery on the below-zero January day.

· · · · ·

My grandfather built barns in eastern Oregon. People still speak about him in words as well formed, as keen and lasting as his barns. They say a rancher would explain exactly the kind of barn he needed. Notes of dimensions, dates, bills of lading fill nickel tablets. No drawings.

Before the rock foundation was laid they say he cut all the boards out on the ground, all the beams, supports, rafters, stacks and piles of hewn timbers and planks. When the materials were ready, he began. A barn lived in his head as music might.

Every job meant a family journey into the forest of old trees and Grandfather's search for one that could be properly milled into a barn. I have a photograph of him standing beside a cut tree with a girth as high as his head. Already middle-aged and yet, he is as lean as a boy. He holds the lines of a white horse he called Robin and the four eldest of Grandfather's children sit holding each other at the waist. Robin pulled the wagon loaded down with supplies and children to the mountain camp, and snaked logs through the heavy stand to a landing. Grandmother ran the camp, caring for the babies, washing and cooking as she did at home. The older children picked huckleberries or currants or elderberries into lard cans when they weren't occupied gathering firewood or helping their

father. For weeks they lived with the smoke of campfire on their skin and fed on the fruit of mountain thickets and streams. Their voices filled the woods like birdsong lifting above the thump of the axe, whining saw, the whetting stone biting a knife-edge into steel. When Grandfather cried, "Timber!" they were hushed by the melancholy sigh of the giant tree falling, breaking through brush and limbs to the ground, and the cleft of silence afterward as the consort of trees adjusted to new light.

Of his eight children all but two are gone now. He and Grandmother are gone too, of course. There was a funeral in the hometown for one of those children on the white horse. Afterward, with a sketched out map, I drove through neighborhoods looking for homes Grandfather built. At first I needed the guide of numbers on the curb. Then I found I could recognize his houses tucked among others as I could the family nose or the family laugh among strangers at the gathering in the park. Grandfather's houses had the unattested lines of prairie style. Elegantly spare. I didn't need a map.

I drove to the country beyond town to find his barns. The road took a sharp turn around a cut and when it straightened one of his barns faced me. I stopped. I stood at the fence holding the wire. Grandfather was standing before me. Not hunched, as he was the only time I remember seeing him. Not shuffling. Not mute. It was the man in the photograph beside the thick tree and his horse named Robin, and his four oldest children.

When I asked my mother why he stopped building she said he wanted to be a rancher, to have his own place and his own barn. Raise cows and calves. Put up some hay. Plant a big garden. Let the chickens run after grasshoppers and lay eggs with orange yolks.

They bought a place on Butter Creek and a new-fangled tractor. Robin was turned out to graze the rest of his days. While farming a steep side-hill the tractor rolled. Grandfather was thrown off and the tractor crushed him. He lay out all day before Grandmother missed him. The hospital kept him a long time. When Uncle Harold brought him home Grandmother placed her canary cage beside his chair hoping the flash of their gold wings and songs might interest him.

I was six when we went for a visit. Grandfather sat in the morning room after breakfast. I had never seen birds in a cage where you could stand close and see their round, black eyes and their throats swell with song. But when I got near, Grandfather made sounds like a hog chuffing or a door being pulled off its hinges, and he reached for me with fingers like claws and arms that couldn't unfold to hold a quick yellow-haired girl.

As a young man in Virginia, Grandfather had taught penmanship to school-children. In our family Bible each stroke recording births and deaths is exact in pressure, cadence, extending to roll the round of vowels, the spike of consonants. No frivolous loops. Nothing just for show. He would apply these same spare techniques to architecture in another place. Joining letters into a word, into an idea, into a theme, was the language of mastering wood into wall. His hand touched every piece fell, milled, shaped, braced, drove the wooden pegs in, lifted it aloft. Foundations sound, centerline plumb, mortises tight as if the timbers grew as one, his barns remain.

I was one life removed from the guidance of Grandfather's hands. If I thought of him at all he was at a distance, dilapidated as an abandoned barn settling into the earth, shingles picked away by wind, spine swayed by time. Growing up moved me further from the man who could not speak and nearer to the point of recognizing his genius. In time I learned to hear the music of his barns, and love changed the memory. In my mind he became a whole and healed man.

Barns smell of more than fodder, more than animals loafing. They smell of pine and cedar and uprights of juniper cut in winter when sap has pulled to the heart so they will stand and not rot. They smell of meadow hay drying, alfalfa, oat hay, barley, and straw put up for bedding. Tin ticks when it heats and tightens when it cools. Children swing on a rope, in and out of light. In the dusk an owl slips from shadowed rafters and sails downfield. End of winter the hay is all fed out; chaff is raked from the floor and hauled away; horse stalls are cleaned and the manure used for dams to turn irrigation water toward dry fields. The empty mow is a place hired men can back a wagon needing repairs, oil harness, or mend tools during spring storms, and when the woman and the choregirl bring coffee and sweet things from the house midmorning, they all lounge and talk and tease and laugh.

First of June we begin cutting hay. By fair-time in late summer we should be done; cow hay yarded and stacked outside; horse hay put inside. Good storms make a good feed year and hay enough to carry us through. When winter draws down from the mountain and my breath is a haze about me, I go to the barn for evening chores. Field cats pace the sill and mew for a handout now that ground squirrels are hibernating and mice are nesting deep in the hay. The haymow is a larder like our cellar shelves of summer fruit in crystalline jars, bins of potatoes, green and gold squash, and carrots heeled down in sand. My buckskin mare and her dun filly are in their stalls. I pull a bale from the stack, break the twine and carry hay to the manger. While they eat I brush the filly and think of days ahead. It is in such beauty I revisit all the horses I have ridden in my life and I know peace in their company.

Grandfather left no pouch of gold. Riches were the bounty of his imagination and the thrifty use of trees cast by simple tools to create a symbol of community serving both neighbor and beast. He gave me barns, beautiful and lasting. As long as his barns stand on open ground, Grandfather stands. As long as his barns stand, I stand also.

19

# The Barn Where It Belongs   *Paul F. Starrs*

The barnyard is a feature not generally looked on with any great favor by people of good taste and exalted refinement. Consider the asperity that greets barnyard language, barnyard behavior, barnyard animals, barnyard wit, barnyard lust. Or for that matter, likely none of us, regardless of age, can fail to recollect the accusatory words, "your room looks like a barnyard." Whether the theme at hand is barn or barnyard, the negative implications conjure something common, disordered, sprawling, uncouth, invoking a near-chaos. Which just goes to show how wrong we can be, for few features of everyday life are so innately deserving of interest as the barnyard and its contents. We see barns, we laud them, we capture them on photographic images as the grain and gristle of an agricultural operation, and in those acts the barn in its setting comes to be with us for life.

The tension is palpable betwixt the all-enveloping barnyard and the noble barn, prideful and standalone. The relationship is deliciously complex: Barn and barnyard are not the same, though they share ideas, some function, and both site and situation. But the barnyard has added utilitarian significance: It can be regarded from any side, and the payoff's a good one. There's more to see around the barnyard, much as a public square is innately more interesting than buildings that sit mutely on the quadrangle. For anyone who cherishes the labor performed on farms and ranches the barnyard assumes added weight: It's the place where much of the real work around an outfit is done.

More than the place where barns are built, the barnyard's vernacular space has important charm, offering an organizational principle to ranch and to farm. The barn sits in the yard, but it is by no means the only thing there. From the camera's viewfinder, true, most images of barns are recorded from a photographer's vantage point in the barnyard — and therefore, the barnyard serves, in effect, as an admiring viewer's point of entry (Figure 1). In fact, that view from the barnyard opening is so standardized as to be almost cliché: How common is it for a barn to be photographed from directly overhead in an aerial view, or from the backside of the barn? Rare indeed.

## The Setting

So it's barn and the barnyard, edifice and setting, peas in a pod. The barn is a respectable part of an agricultural operation, though not as much so as the house, always the domain of the female head of household. Even given that level of domestication, the barn building has long been a kind of storage area, a repository for useful items whose best and highest purposes have not yet necessarily been determined, but which are recognized as being useful, at some time in the future. The barn is, in that regard, akin to certain seldom used kitchen cupboards, or perhaps like the top dresser drawer of most men. Such is their supreme flexibility. For a barn, setting is almost every-

Figure 1: The barnyard is a receptive place. This example, in the Oasis Ranch along the California-Nevada border, in Fish Lake Valley, shows much of the cordial chaos of the successful barnyard. At back left is one of the old stone storage buildings; a trailer, long stationary, is opposite that. Caterpillar tractors, tractor-pulled farm implements, and even an inside-out tire, used for keeping livestock feed off the ground, is in the foreground. And rising above all are the cottonwoods, the symbol of any mature Western ranch — and ranch yard. (Photo by Paul F. Starrs, May 1987)

Figure 2: Along the old U.S. 40 route, now bypassed by a more modern highway, lies the Carroll Canyon Ranch, with its buildings pleasingly laid out and visible to the passer-by. There is on this and many a ranch an intergenerational order and symmetry, from the old stone buildings dug into the hillside, to the outhouses and potato storage sheds, to the barn and fenced yard. This sweep of life is typical of the layout of the working ranch: a versatile, or fungible, space that can be put to many uses, yet maintain an elegant facade to the ranch. (Photo by Paul F. Starrs, June 1997)

thing. The "almost" is appropriate because barns, like garages, are sometimes put to other, unintended, uses, and it is this very flexibility that makes the barn particularly attractive, whether for agriculture, photography, or architectural studies. Because a barn starts out life as one thing certainly doesn't mean it will end up so. The same is true of its place: The barn belongs in the barnyard. But the barnyard is by far the rangier locale.

The barnyard is blessed with a fungibility that is com-

parable to — possibly even greater than — the barn's. Getting the right perspective on this is important: In touring ranches and farms, I have learned that verticality matters (as did nineteenth-century recorders of bird's-eye view maps). Unless a light plane is right at hand, farms aren't easy to rise above, but ranches have a great virtue of often lying at the edge of meadows, with roads rising nearby them. Come across the crest, drive along a road, or hike up a hill, and below proves to be

21

the barnyard (Figure 2). The layout and the drama of the barnyard can be seen from afar, which is a virtue, since for those who are building-oriented, getting inside a barn isn't always so easy. Fieldwork associated with barns involves considerable contact with the owners or manager, who aren't necessarily sympathetic. Barnyards are easier to acquire in good perspective, though. They are there for the viewing with a great and overt geometry.

The direction of farm and ranch domestic space was once undeniably focused at the barn building, itself. But that was a kind of founder's folly, a mistake. Scattered through a dozen, sixty, or a hundred years of time about the barn are innumerable expressions of life and work. There is a virtue to this — from even a close-by elevated view, the barnyard beckons, a cordial mess. Parked there are fifty-year-old tractors, not worth hauling to the implement dealer, and not yet ready to be contributed to the town's historical museum, as "antique farm equipment" for an appallingly small tax write-off. The barnyard serves as a kind of a commons, open to all, but demanding of no special service.

While barns are rather specific creations architecturally, which can be categorized according to such intricacies as their gables, their roofing materials, their bays and their building stuffs, the barnyard is much less era-specific. It's a worksite, a *tabula rasa* where labors can be performed, like a barn's concrete flooring, and it is versatile and adaptable space, like the asphalt pad at a drive-in movie venue that's sometimes campus to a *concours d'elegance,* and at other times site of a swap meet. Yards are open-access goods, where things happen. And that is one of the fine qualities to barnyards: they hold the past, are open to projects, welcoming the future. They've been many things to almost anyone; they are anonymous but eminently serviceable space. Many of us find that laudable. The barn is a kind of high culture, a small taste of establishment art. But the barnyard has none of that. It's space waiting for purpose. I've known barnyards that are storage sites; barnyards in which the open hard-packed dirt is where a grain harvest is dropped and then winnowed; I've seen barnyards where every farm and ranch vehicle has been repaired, with the ground so resilient that it supports mechanics' creepers that run back and forth under the chassis of the temporarily broken down archaic pickups that are a mainstay of work on ranch or farm. Barnyards are where old vehicles are parked, die, and settle, becoming one with the ground. They have their virtue.

**Making the Barn Work**

Sixty years ago, when hay was harvested loose and stacked or sheaved by hand, the barn was a crucial meeting point where carefully gathered grain and feed, essential livestock, storage, and human workers convened. In the bower of the barn, grass or alfalfa cut on a pasture was drawn upward by pulley to a hayloft to become stored fodder. Resting in the barn, the animals that provided the motive power of an operation (horses, mules, even oxen) would escape the elements and lounge in heavy wood stalls. And, in the lower reaches of the barn would be performed work that was too exacting to do outside in inclement weather. The barn was home to varied jobs: leather tooling and harness repair, doctoring the horses and draft stock, even a spot of playing and goofing-off for community children. A barn was, therefore, a kind of pivot and supply point for the rest of the ranch. That was then. Since, and for this reason old barns are often found picturesque, many a barn has fallen to disrepair. Hay is not harvested loose, now, but into string- and wire-bound bales: rarely 80-pounders, sometimes 150 pound rectangles, often 1000 pound square bales, or where hay is winter fodder that need not travel far, it is rolled into behemoth round bales weighing a clean ton each: 2200 pounds. For this reason alone, in the twenty-first century, wooden barns tightly subdivided for stalls and storage just aren't so useful; or, at least, their uses are a far cry from anything barns were originally built to do. Attractive anachronisms, in most circumstances barns are like the buildings of a preserved ghost town, maintained only to a state of "arrested decay." More often, the weathered wood barn slowly topples in mute testament to gravity's authority and to a gentle relaxing of the grip of hand-made nails or pins that were once pounded home with much authority. The travel and direction is all earthward. And since we're all bound there, someday, per-

haps we need not pity the poor barn.

Barns were home to remarkable collaborations of humans and animals. The novelist John Berger once wrote a book about life among French peasants in the nineteenth and early twentieth centuries, titling it *Pig Earth,* and that book's a good reminder of just how intertwined people, livestock, and barns once were. In rural life, the barn was shelter from the storms, superior as a windbreak; for animals a home, for humans a haven. Inside its eaves calves were born and bottle-fed, swine farrowed, colts conceived. Silage, when fed to dairy stock, would have the heady smell reminiscent of hops, but always redolent of something beer-like and improved-upon and rich. These encounters of building and stock and humans were — and in some places still are — part of the cycle of agricultural production. Rural people knew about it, and in their own way relished all that. City people did not, could not, would not be able to recognize the barn as something that made all this possible. Barns were the emblems of respectable domesticity. They are something else, now; something more nostalgic than working: akin now to anything else that was once a staple of ranch or farm life that has gone Gucci-chic, like the yuppie pickup truck, or cowboy boots that will never be covered with cow shit, leather chaps reserved for gay-pride parades or a cadre of dykes-on-bikes; tractors miniaturized for mowing the south quarter-acre of lawn, or even the great cast-iron wood-fired stove, once the mainstay of a home-canning operation, but now a nicely fancy collectible.

What would be the ideal barn now? In his book *True Stories,* it is the timeless admonition of David Byrne, lead mind of the *Talking Heads,* that these days the perfect structure would have to be a manufactured metal building: versatile, high-roofed, durable yet easily repaired, movable when desired, and all but immune to fire. But the artistic admirers of metal buildings are in fact few. Maybe functionality isn't everything; there are those who still love the grain of wood and a barn's archaic contents. In a recent drive through Wyoming, Utah, and Nevada, where in rural spots agriculture is still a matter taken seriously, I was reminded of the militant discrepancy between what's eye-catching and what's cost-effective. If the wooden barn in these days is so pricey that it is rarely built, or even repaired, its higher virtues would have to be counted as aesthetic rather than apparent. The barn remains the harbinger of a certain kind of special space. Others may write about the architecture and private lives of barns; I like barns as partial documents of the larger received ranch.

**The Versatile Barn**
Although the barnyard is clearly my favorite part of an outfit, it's beyond argument that a barn will include something of interest to nearly anyone. Some love the notches in log-constructed traditional barns; others applaud barn design. Some love the grain of the old wood; others the stoutness of the vertical barn supports, run high so the roof is well supported by an echelon of single uprights, and the upper spaces can lie secure. Some love the hex signs, others the hay lofts, with their salacious and secretive memories. Who, after all, can ever forget Flannery O'Connor's "Good Country People," when, after a barn encounter of a particularly Southern Gothic nature, the Bible salesman (Manly Pointer, a name too good to be made up) zings the ultimate knowing parting shot: "One time I got a woman's glass eye this way." Or think back to all the films in which barns loom, from *Oh Brother, Where Art Thou?* to *Arachnaphobia* to *Belizaire: The Cajun*, to *Songcatcher* to *Witness.* In each, the barn is a triumphant part of the landscape.

Why is it that barns so much augur possibility, refuge, solace, sanctuary, and promise? Literally rooted, their structural members designed to withstand generations of stacked bales, leaning horses, and the chance violent encounter with wayward farm equipment, it is barns that signal commitment to a spot (Figure 3). A family that erected a barn had to be willing to pour capital into what historically was the second most expensive building on a rural property — and in more than a few cases, the barn was far more expensive to build than the original farm or ranch house, since that was put up with a minimum of resources, and when a barn was constructed, it was as a signature and symbol of stability. There is a great contrast of inside and outside in the barn, too.

Figure 3: The yard, even on a grain and hay ranch, is an essential bit of space. It provides the entrée to the operation, through badly-hung (or at least sagging) metal gates, and the older barn in the background has not been of really essential use for some years. But the equipment is arrayed about the yard, a gooseneck stock trailer at one side, a swather on another, the loading chute near the barn corrals. Grass grows tall around the buildings, for who has time before fall to cut it, and isn't a profusion of grass a symbol of plenty that might someday avert want. The town of Upalco, Utah, is hardly a pivot of agricultural success, but this ranch is clearly holding its own. (Photo by Paul F. Starrs, July 2002)

The outside was for all; inside barns were where things could happen that were best reserved out of sight, crucial settings for film, for portraiture, for community.

The word "community" is much of what barns are all about. The Western films of the 1940s and 1950s were replete with community barn-raisings; part of the celluloid past, admittedly, but those scenes were included in movies because the United States was in recovery from some parlous times, and film directors and screenwriters wanted to include, on film, a symbol of people working together toward a common, visible, and palpable goal. That was putting up a barn, and as rare as those events probably were, their symbolism still permeates the buildings. Barns were reflections of where people were from; their architecture an accumulation of knowledge that was brought from other distant spots. The notches, the design, the girders, the wood-shaping techniques, were not "American," they were Danish or German or Spanish or Mexican or Bavarian or Scots, which is to say, they were as American as anything could be: put together from diverse parts. The barn, as planned and built, was an expression of local skills and knowledge.

Today, barns are living archives of changing times, changing production, changing labor, changing needs. Almost no one, in this day and age, uses horses for routine farm work; therefore, the use of the barn as shelter and housing is an anachronism. Tractors aren't often stored in barns; they're parked in the barnyard. When they are replaced with a newer model, sometimes the old one is hauled away, sometimes not, but the barn is not really a factor in their survival or use.

Whether the barn serves any enduring practical use remains to be seen. There are few places where livestock are wintered in barns, now. Once, purebred stock was feared delicate, and a Shorthorn bull or an Angus cow would be sheltered through the winter months, almost anyplace in the northern half of the United States. But, in an odd twist in our sybaritic twenty-first century culture, livestock are much less pampered now than 150 or even 50 years ago; they are expected to make their own living on the range. There are cleaner, less difficult to maintain alternatives to wooden barns, and these modern facilities can be heated and cooled more readily than the structures forged of local materials. The needs are different, and so are the buildings that accommodate farm and ranch existence. Records aren't kept in notches on the wall, they are maintained in spreadsheets on computers, and those require somewhat more sanitary, climate-controlled, and less dusty circumstances than offered by the average barn. Still, we admire the barn as we might anything tested by time.

## Showcasing Barns

I like barns because of their connections to the world around. Barns are where things are done on many an outfit, and as a property changes in the orbit of a barn, the utility of the building, its functions and wherewithal, change too. Investigate what the barn is being used for, and you learn what is going on all about.

But another delight of the barn is the way it holds and showcases past uses; since few of us lay claim to the demonic energy needed to clean out a barn, especially given the risks of maladies like hanta virus, they are structures we tend to leave well enough alone. The record preserved in a barn isn't stratigraphic, sorted top-to-bottom, like the geological time table; instead, a barn demonstrates its history through stacking: it lives on with its bundles of equipment, old saddles, moldering hay, empty Omolene grain sacks, jars of balms and disinfectants, including what is invariably referred to as "gentian violet," ritually employed in the doctoring of sore livestock feet. Owls may frequent the rafters (they keep down the numbers of the mice and rats, which go with the relict stores of grain and fodder). The barn contains exquisite cumulations of nests and webs and burlap bags and folded and wrapped ovals of baling wire, all stashed for future use in mangers and stalls that haven't been used in forty years, not since a tri-wheel tractor replaced the unmatched pair of Belgian draft horses.

The barn is life. The barnyard is crucial to its presentation. Together, these are not just interesting features, they are testaments to our relationship to the rural land. Of course, fewer than one-quarter of one-percent of Americans are "farmers," in 2000. There may be more barns now than actual farm dwellers; the count would at least be a close one. But that is nothing to fear or lament. It is, instead, the reality of twenty-first century living. In the overwhelmingly urban American West, we may still cherish our barns, for they do signify what we were, and that is nothing to be feared.

# Timber Frame Barns of Carson Valley     *Paul Oatman*

The barns on the eastern slope of the Sierra Nevada represent the last hurrah of a building system whose roots go back to between 200 and 500 B. C. The first temples of Greece were built of wood. In the first century B.C., Vitruvius described the construction, calling it *opus craticiom*, or "timber framing." Timber framing consists of timbers fastened together with mortise and tenon joints and secured with wooden pins. It took a firm hold in the Far East and Northern Europe, culminating in the hammerbeam roof of Westminster Hall, London, built by Master Hugh Herland, carpenter, from 1394 to 1400 (J. H. Harvey, *The Master Builders*, London, 1971). Harvey describes Westminster Hall as "the greatest single work of art of the whole of the European Middle Ages." It has a clear span of a little more than 67 feet and covers an area almost half an acre. The earliest English settlers and other ethnic groups that followed transported timber framing to America. It was the dominant building system for houses until about 1840. Then the combined factors of the mass production of nails, proliferation of sawmills, a booming population, major urban fires, westward expansion, and a lack of skilled craftsmen produced today's stick frame houses. Yet barns and other large structures such as railroad depots continued to be timber framed until the 1920s.

The building of a timber frame sawmill by James Marshall, employed by John Sutter, was the catalyst of the California Gold Rush. (Gold was discovered in the river while the sawmill was being constructed.) As westward migration increased, timber framing was brought to a new land. The fertile valleys along the eastern slopes of the Sierra Nevada Mountains sprouted barns to store the hay for ranches and to shelter dairy cows and work animals. Many of these utilitarian structures that were built between 1850 and 1920 survive today. Historians and scholars have ignored these buildings for too long. Trophy houses are displacing ranches in some areas, such as Carson Valley, at such a rapid rate that the need to record these icons is more imperative than ever.

Because of the scant attention paid to these buildings they have been lumped into a category called the western or prairie barn, a term which is too general to be accurate. Through eight years of research, I have come to believe that the barns of the eastern slopes of the Sierra Nevada constitute a unique subtype, which I call the Nevada Barn. With illustrations I will describe the findings of my research.

The Nevada Barns I have studied, from north of Reno through the Carson Valley and into adjacent valleys in California, appear to be of a Lowland origin, Dutch and German. An early example is in Diamond Valley, just over the California border from Genoa, known at that time as Dutch Valley. The secondary tie beams in this barn were marked "Dutch Valley" with crayon. This barn has tapered rafters which are a common feature of Dutch barns. The massive anchor beam has been displaced by a 12 by 12 inch dropped tie beam. The dropped tie beam, a tie beam which is below the top plate, is a common feature in the two hundred or so barns I have inspected.

Nevada Barns also share other common features. A Jackson Hayfork, a device for loading hay into the barn from an opening at the top of the gable, runs on a track along the nave or center aisle. All the frames are fastened with softwood pins, and foot braces on posts are common, no doubt a necessity to deal with high winds, as in a "Washoe Zephyr." Posts lacking foot bracing have 6 inch tenons, usually double pinned to the 12 by 12 ground plate or groundsill. Only two roof shapes were used. One is a gable roof, usually at a 9 in 12 pitch, and the other is a gable roof over the central aisle with side aisles having shed roofs, or, more poetically, "wings." The majority of barns have a central aisle for hay and side aisles for livestock. Some larger barns, like the Van Sickle barn outside Genoa, have principal purlin posts (see diagram, page 30) to support the 32 foot span of the central aisle. The central aisle had no door since hay was loaded with the Jackson Hayfork from the opening at the top of the gable. Openings were later cut in the walls for tractors. Some barns had a side entry into the central bay through which the hay wagon could drive. The Dressler barn in the Carson Valley is a fine example of a side entry barn.

The layout and assembly of Nevada barns are worthy of note. Nevada's earliest barns (built in the1850s) have long purlins and eave plates, both of which are hand hewn, some measuring 60 feet long with only one scarf joint (Figure 1) in their entire length. The Van Sickle barn has an extremely unusual scarf joint and is the only one fastened with wooden pins. All other barns have scarf joints held with steel bolts. The scarf joint is the key to which side the barn was erected from. The bottom of the scarf joint indicated which side the layout started from, that is, the piece with the bottom was put down first. All frames are "square rule." This is an American layout system in which rough lumber is sized to a common number along both height and width (Figures 2 and 3). For example, an 8 by 8 inch timber may measure 8 and 1/4 or 7 and 3/4 so the builder cuts all his timbers for 7 and 1/2. Thereby all the braces become interchangeable.

The ground sills were laid first and were usually 12 by 12 inch timbers, the largest in the frame and in most cases hand hewn even after 1900. These large timbers were needed to support the frame and rested on piers of rock. Next, the central aisle was assembled in a series of "bents" or sections. The purlin or aisle posts and braces were put into place, then the dropped tie beam was added. Each bent was raised, connected with interties and a purlin plate was fitted on top of the bents. The outer side aisle walls were built as one "wall bent" and connected to the main frame with secondary tie beams. A common rafter roof system was built last and united the structure. Finally, all frames were "draw bored." Pinholes in the mortise were laid out approximately 1 and 1/2 to 2 inches from the edge of the timber where a 1 inch hole was bored. The tenon is laid out the same but set back 1/8th to 3/16th of an inch closer to the shoulder of the tenon so that the joint is pulled tight when the pin is driven in. This is also why all the pins are pointed.

There is as much mystery as history to these huge barns.

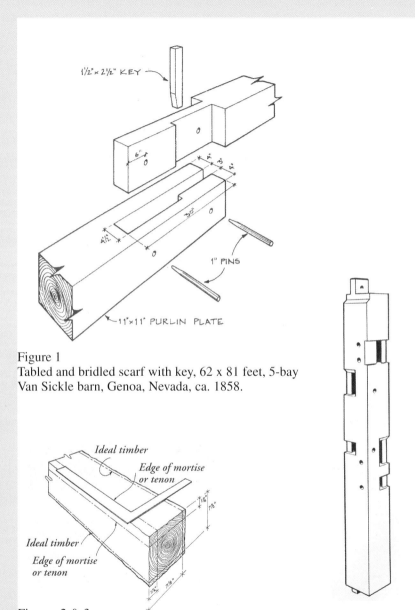

**Figure 1**
Tabled and bridled scarf with key, 62 x 81 feet, 5-bay
Van Sickle barn, Genoa, Nevada, ca. 1858.

**Figures 2 & 3**
English framers, who worked with short or crooked timber, used a layout
system called scribe rule. American framers, using long, straight trees, used a
method called square rule, which is illustrated here.

There is in particular scant information concerning the builders. In 1999, I interviewed Richard Gansberg of Foothill Road outside of Genoa, who was ninety at the time, and he informed me that his hand hewn barn was built in 1910 by a master carpenter named William Thran and that the beams were hewed by Henry Arnett, a member of the Washoe Tribe. Gansberg's saw-milled barn was built in 1914 by Henry Manke. Rancher Joe Schneider of Jack's Valley has three timber frame barns, the one illustrated (page 31) being a fine example of a Nevada Barn, well built with no frills. He also has the only double pen & drive ("dog trot") barn I have seen. This is a log barn with hand hewn logs, one 67 feet long! This barn is not traditional timber-frame construction; rather the squared logs are stacked and notched at the ends in a manner similar to a traditional log cabin. Schneider's grandfather told him that it was built by Chinese workers in 1850. The Van Sickle Barn harbors a peculiar scarf joint that seems to be of French origin. It is included in Jack Sobon's *Historic American Timber Joinery, A Graphic Guide.* This book, which was funded by a grant from the National Center for Preservation Technology and Training (of the U.S. National Park Service) can be down loaded from the Timber Framers Guild web site at *www.tfguild.org.* Sobon's hand drawn illustrations of joinery clearly show that a picture is worth a thousand words. Again, I cannot emphasize enough the need to record these icons now, because McDonald's, Walmart and Blockbuster are coming through the barn door.

29

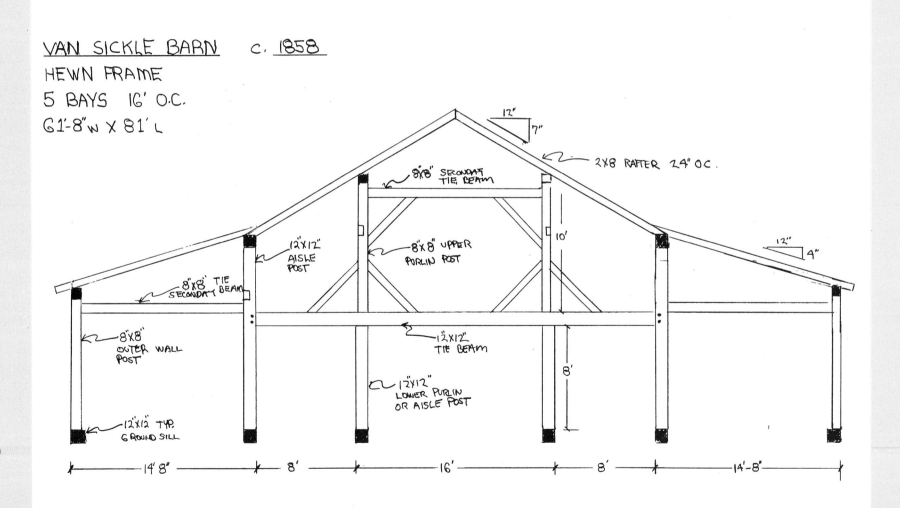

VAN SICKLE BARN    c. 1858
HEWN FRAME
5 BAYS   16' O.C.
61'-8"W X 81' L

12"
7"

2X8 RAFTER 24" O.C.

8"X8" SECONDAY
TIE BEAM

8"X8" UPPER
PURLIN POST

10'

12"
4"

12"X12"
AISLE
POST

8"X8" TIE
SECONDAY BEAM

12"X12"
TIE BEAM

8"X8"
OUTER WALL
POST

8'

12"X12"
LOWER PURLIN
OR AISLE POST

12"X12" TYP.
GROUND SILL

14' 8"        8'          16'          8'        14'-8"

30

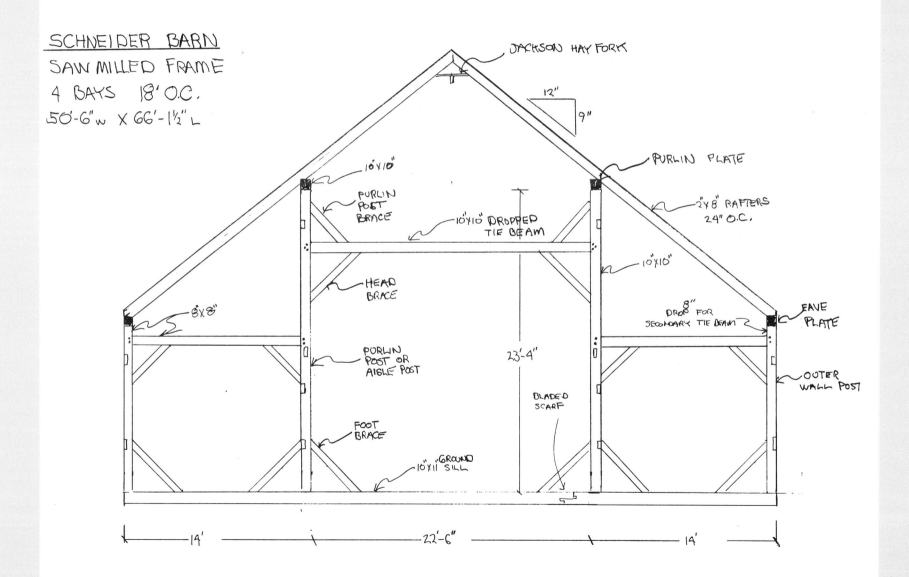

SCHNEIDER BARN
SAW MILLED FRAME
4 BAYS 18' O.C.
50'-6"w X 66'-1½"L

JACKSON HAY FORK

12"
9"

PURLIN PLATE

10"x10"

PURLIN POST BRACE

2"x8" RAFTERS 24" O.C.

10"x10" DROPPED TIE BEAM

10"x10"

HEAD BRACE

8"x8"

23'-4"

DROP 8" FOR SECONDARY TIE BEAM

EAVE PLATE

PURLIN POST OR AISLE POST

OUTER WALL POST

FOOT BRACE

BLADED SCARF

10"x11" "GROUND" SILL

14'

22'-6"

14'

31

# Glossary of Timber-Frame Terms

**anchor beam**
The major tying beam in a Dutch barn.

**beam**
A horizontal timber that may run either lengthwise or crosswise.

**brace**
A subsidiary member set diagonally to strengthen a timber frame.

**draw bore**
After the mortise is cut, a hole is bored in the mortise squarely through both cheeks. This measurement is transferred to the tenon, then offset $1/8^{th}$ to $3/16^{ths}$ inch toward the shoulder of the tenon. A wooden pin is then driven through these holes and, by forcing them in line, it brings the shoulders of the tenon tight up against the cheeks of the mortise making the joint firm.

**dropped tie beam**
A tie beam below the top plate, and put in place first.

**eave plate**
Also called top plate or capping plate. Horizontal longitudinal member which extends over outside wall posts and whose upper face supports the seat cut of the rafters.

**ground plate** or **groundsill**
The first horizontal member laid for a timber-frame building.

**hammerbeam**
Horizontal bracket projecting at a wall plate level on opposite sides of the wall like a tie beam with the center cut away. The inner ends carry vertical timbers called hammer posts and braces to a collar beam.

**Jackson Hayfork**
A device for picking up hay from outside of the barn, and transporting it along the ridgepole to an appropriate place inside using a roller and track system.

**mortise and tenon**
A joint formed by a projecting piece (or tenon) fitting into a socket (or mortise), usually both square cut.

**pin**
A small piece of wood, cut in the direction of the fibers and sharpened on one end, used to hold together the parts of a mortise and tenon joint.

**post**
A main vertical member that supports either a wall or a roof, often both.

**purlin plate**
A horizontal (parallel to the ground) longitudinal (running the length of the barn in the same direction as the ridge piece) member in a roof system that supports the rafters.

**scarf joint**
A joint made by notching, grooving, or otherwise cutting the ends of two pieces and fastening them so that they lap over and join firmly into one continuous piece.

**tie beam**
A transverse horizontal member that spans from wall to wall or eave to eave, resisting the outward thrust of the roof plates,

**timber**
A large squared or dressed piece of wood.

# Surveying the Visual   *Peter Goin*

This story begins in the late summer of the first year of a new millennium. Under cool lights on a hot August afternoon, students gather in a university classroom. Only days before, I had challenged every one of them that their work would occupy a place in Nevada's history—*if they rose to the occasion!* "How often," I asked, "…does any artist have an opportunity to know—in advance—that their work will be saved for posterity?" The thought that what they were about to begin would result in a significant collaborative document, a substantial archive, is both wonderful and sobering at the same time. Regardless of my challenge, the photographs must endure for their own intrinsic value, for the quality of the craft and of the vision, and because of the breadth of the collaborative effort. Yet it is worth noting that these are undergraduate students early in their photographic training, untested in professional arenas. On this day, these students were offered an opportunity to bear witness to Nevada's changing rural agricultural landscape.

But we did not have much time. In a mere two months, the majority of the fieldwork was scheduled for completion. Immediately, therefore, intense lectures, presentations and discussions commenced with Ron James, Historic Preservation Officer for the State of Nevada, and with Paul Oatman, timber-frame scholar and artisan. The students learned about the Timber Framers Guild of North America and received a copy of the Historic Wooden Structure Archives Survey Checklist—this a very detailed list of how to record timber structures, down to the riven and pegs of timber-to-log conversion. We also spoke broadly about the Farm Security Administration (FSA) photographs, including strategies, script lists, and problems in the field. The students realized that despite a few excellent studies, little is really known about Nevada ranch structures and the culture that created them. Nevada's ranch architecture is culturally complex, deriving from such varied populations as Italian, Basque, and German. The materials and techniques used in rural Nevada architecture are often distinctive in their adaptation to scarce resources.

Soon, the students were studying the assignment sheets. These sheets were generalized working scripts, listing contact information for owners and caretakers as well as a few interesting historical facts about rural architecture on ranch properties. The sites selected ranged from railroad tie sheds near Elko to divorce ranches in Clark County. These assignment sheets clearly referenced the more formalized and heavily detailed scripts typically provided to Dorothea Lange, Russell Lee, Arthur Rothstein, and other government photographers by Roy Stryker, Director of the Historical Section of the FSA. The students' assignment sheets were absolutely essential as the initial point of departure into the landscape.

Working groups emerged and the cacophony of voices reflected the choices made. Catana Barnes sought out the old stone brick house and barn located on the property of the Jones Ranch in Washoe County. She also photographed extensively on the property of the Twaddle Pedroli Ranch. Laura Fillmore, Amber Martin, and Andrea Martinez claimed Churchill County, with a list containing contact information for the Kallenbach barn, the Moiola Ranch barn, the Kent Ranch and the Wightman Ranch, among others. On the list were the Cushman potato cellar, the Alpine Ranch Barn, the Oakden House, and the Harriman Barns. Andrea investigated the Lattin Farms Single Faced Barn in Fallon, learning that Mr. Lattin thought that this was the oldest barn in the Valley. He was not able to move the barn in one piece from its original location, so they dismantled it and then reassembled it on this property. Since then, they have decided to use the east and west walls in the construction of a contemporary barn, for a more authentic look. The new barn they are constructing will be used for events and for selling produce. Andrea also photographed on the Alpine Ranch and a water tower on the Seven Hanging Hearts Ranch.

Douglas County, including Genoa, Minden, and the Carson Valley was attractive to more students—Aimee Lopes, Ryan Quinlan, Micah Silva-Frank, Jessica Slack, Laura Fillmore, Tsunaki Tabayashi, and Ikue Yada. That two Japanese photographers have joined our survey adds another layer of significance to the project. Tsunaki visited rural Nevada for the first time, documenting the beautiful red barn on the property of the Teig Ranch in Carson Valley. He also traveled to the Lovelock area, photographing the Arino, List and Monroe ranches. On their Carson Valley list was the Dressler Ranch with several barns on the

property, some interesting outbuildings, and a lovely older home, the Giovacchini property, and the Frey/Trimmer House built in 1885 by Lawrence Frey. This is the house where schoolteachers were often boarded, and where Ikue photographed. There she learned that the Frey Ranch was located on 'Land Claim No.1' which they had purchased from John Reese, the first settler and founder of Mormon Station, later named Genoa. The Heitman House Barn, owned by Joe and Michelle Smaltz, was originally situated in Gardnerville. It was built in 1890 and moved to Genoa in 1975. Also on the list were the Hansen Ranch and the Settlemeyer Ranch with nine historic buildings between them. During March, 1940, Arthur Rothstein (FSA) had selectively photographed the Dangberg Ranch in Minden, also on the list. Aimee also spent considerable time closer to home in Reno, photographing the Gray Ranch that was built before the turn of the century, but never officially dated. This property was previously owned by Charlie "Two-Gun" Ferrell, a local sheriff who gained notoriety due to his alleged involvement in the deaths of many American Indians. Aimee photographed the Byington and Williams ranches in Genoa and the Dressler, Hanson, and Scossa ranches in Carson Valley. Ryan captured the smokehouse on the Burr Family Ranch and made a number of photographs of timber-frame construction. He also documented the grain thresher and stone creamery at the Henry Van Sickle Station on the Teig Family Ranch in Genoa. While Jessica traveled with other members of the group, she focused principally on the Hennigson, the

White, and the Hellwinkel barns in Gardnerville. Chris Hellwinkel's grandfather built their barn in 191i, but it has half a new roof, so half the roof is metal and the other half is wood shingles.

The prepared lists—photographic scripts, if you will— were not a complete collection of all the ranches in Nevada. Visiting each ranch would be an overwhelming undertaking. What the students needed was a *beginning*, a place to start, a contact person, and a methodology for initiating the fieldwork. Having said this, the nineteen single-spaced pages enumerated many wonderful properties through all of Nevada's counties. Students were also encouraged to seek out structures or properties not listed, but to remember the importance of maintaining a proper and professional manner at all times. Rural architecture is alive, in a state of change. Students were encouraged to seek images that told part of the story of rural life. "Conduct yourself in a manner that reflectes the fundamental seriousness of the assignment, of the project itself." Financial accountability was expected, as each student received a small stipend for materials and travel. At the end of the project, each student was asked to provide a minimum of fifteen 8" x 10" gelatin silver prints, archivally processed and printed to fine art standards. This im- plies photographs that reflect a controlled transition between tonal areas, adequate lighting, sufficient clarity of focus, appropriate depth-of-field, no visible dust marks or scratches, a decisive composition, and a consistent printing strategy enabling viewers to recognize and evaluate the subject.

R. Nelson Parrish and Matt Theilen photographed in Lyon County, including Mason Valley and Yerington. They were asked to call on Charles and Bella Warr, Flora Farias, Dean and Cheryl Del Porto, John Poli, Marion Gable, Josephine Manha, Joe and Beverly Landolt, John Ritter, the Capurro, Scatena and Scierini ranches, Reno and Vonnie Aiazzi…well, the list continues but there clearly was not sufficient time to contact everyone. In some cases, the narrow timing of the student's proposed visit was not convenient for the property owners. The fieldwork portion of the project was scheduled for completion by the end of October, in part due to the change of seasons' effect on the visual scene. But there was another reason for this deadline and that was due to the artificial time parameters of a university semester that ends in early December. The students needed darkroom lab time to process their negatives and make contact sheets, essentially creating a positive document of each and every negative exposed. Steve Davis, the liaison with the Nevada Humanities Committee, set up afternoon appointments budgeting twenty minutes per student; he would review the contact sheets and help choose which negatives should be printed. In this way, he served as a 'client director' offering a uniform selection process consistent with the goals and programs of the exhibition. As the professor in charge of the fieldwork and semester coursework, I supervised the students' printing skills, selection process, and final prepara- tion work. Imbued in this process was a regular critique seminar where peers, colleagues and faculty reviewed photographic prints for consistency and accuracy. Within this format, the creative process became increasingly important in complementing rather than duplicating others' work, offering innovative compositional designs, and allowing for experimental visual responses to the traditional documentary photograph.

Students were asked to consider documenting beyond the barn itself, including structures such as smokehouses, corrals, stables, milk houses, granaries, bunkhouses, chicken houses, stone outbuildings, blacksmith shops, tack rooms, and even windmill towers. In a couple of cases, old railroad cars, hay derricks and garages were included. Ryan Quinlan and Miranda Gerlock signed up for the Lovelock area, but Miranda worked alone, photographing the Aufdermaur Barn and on the property of Big Meadow Ranch. Deborah Cruze, Jennifer Ober, Ariana Russell, Arlo Schenk, Anna Schooley, and David Torch offered to work in the vicinity of Elko County. This was a huge assignment, and was separated into Ruby Valley and Lamoille, the North Fork, Tuscarora and the South Fork/Lee/Jiggs areas, Pine Valley, and Halleck.

While some students worked with local guides, others preferred to work alone. While working in Nye County, Deborah was amazed that her guide, Allen Metscher, seemed to know every road, every shortcut, every stranger, every person who had a story to tell from the cow boss at Fish Lake to the ranch hand at Hot Creek to the bartender in Manhattan. Deborah photographed

the wonderful buildings at Moore's Station while Jen Ober photographed the stone-based barn on the Smith's Brothers OX Ranch in Ruby Valley, and accompanied by Anna and Ariana photographed the Barnes and Gardner ranches and the Zaga and Zunino ranches. Ariana also attended to the old barn built in 1873 on the Overland Ranch and photographed on the property of the Spring Mountain Ranch in Clark County. Arlo accompanied Tom Boyer, who together photographed in Midas Valley, down Pleasant Valley Road in Lamoille, the Lee Ranch and the Six Bar Ranch, the Metropolis Barns, Bob's Ranch, and the Pescio Saw Mill, among others. Anna was intrigued by the railroad tie shed on the property of the McMullen Ranch in the Jiggs area. David Torch photographed the Keddy Ranch/Tule Ranch/Upper Tule Ranch managed and owned by Susan Glaser and Peter Church. Originally, the German immigrant Mathias Glaser purchased this entire property for $15,000 in land script. Fulfilling the requirements for thinking 'beyond the barn,' David Torch also photographed outhouses, the decorative wallpaper located in the attic of the home built in 1894 where Susan and Peter Church reside, cabins built of railroad ties, stables, a birdfeeder on the property of the Maggie Creek Ranch, and collapsed houses in Tuscarora.

After reviewing the list, students initiated a discussion about whether it would be appropriate to document the Ruby Valley Pony Express station, circa 1860, moved to the Northeast Nevada Museum in Elko. They also began to categorize the railroad tie sheds, circa 1900, in the Lamoille Canyon area. Laura

Fillmore, specifically due to her work with indigenous language renewal in the Great Basin, asked to photograph in the Owyhee area. As it turned out, she conducted an *ad hoc* collection of stories entitled the "Owyhee and the Hopi Stonemasons," "Barn Survives the Turn of Two Centuries & Bootlegging Before it Begins to Kneel," and a modest oral history of two elders speaking Washiw. She also photographed in the Fallon area, specifically on the property of the Kent Ranch. She made an articulate statement in defense of saving the Moiola Ranch Barn, currently falling in on one side underneath the main floor.

In southern Nevada, Dusty Hartman and Nick Profaizer photographed in and around Panaca and Pioche, extending to the Spring Mountain Ranch, near Red Rock. LaMont Johnson signed up for Moapa Valley and Virgin Valleys. His script included the adobe Huntsman Granary built in 1865 as part of the original Mormon settlement, and a few pioneer-era structures. As often happens in survey fieldwork, LaMont requested this specific area because he realized a personal connection—his wife has pioneering roots in Lincoln and eastern Clark counties and still has relatives living in the area. He proposed a field trip across Highway 50, turning south through Lincoln County and then into Moapa and Virgin valleys. There he photographed the Cement Silo in Bunkerville, structures on the Whitney Ranch, and, of course, the Huntsman Granary. While photographing the old Capalappa Ranch barn in Logandale, LaMont discovered that this is a very old farm building formerly owned by a man named Livingston from Salt Lake City who also owned the Hidden Valley Ranch in Glendale, Nevada. When the Depression hit, the owner went bankrupt, cut the ranch up into small farms, and sold them to help clear the mortgage on his Hidden Valley Ranch. A man named Zubia currently owns this building and surrounding area.

Wally Cuchine, Director of the Eureka Opera House, gave a wonderful guided tour of the area to David Colburn, who took the initiative to create a parallel rephotographic survey of a few of Eureka's historic structures. David discovered reluctance in some ranchers who feared that an official designation of "historic"—with a government imprint—might restrict what they could do with the property. David also photographed on the property of the Melka, New Baumann, and Willow Creek ranches. In a note delivered later to me, David Colborn kindly wrote that this project was "…an opportunity of a lifetime. I would certainly like to participate in any others of a similar nature. I liked being able to work independently yet on a theme in common with others. The goal is always to generate a whole which is greater than the sum of its parts."[1] Deborah Cruze also wrote about the importance of the survey, and learned via her fieldwork that the loss of ranching culture is an "inevitable tragedy." She wrote that "…family ranches do not seem to make money enough to support the present generations who now operate them and the future generations who must learn to operate them if the ranches are to survive."[2] She also worked diligently as a project assistant, including conducting additional photography within Paradise Valley during the fall of 2002.

This project was no small task, demanding countless hours photographing throughout the state of Nevada. Students crisscrossed the state numerous times, in some cases used their own finances essentially subsidizing this section of the entire project, and printed and reprinted in the darkrooms until the professional standards of photographic excellence were met. Many of the students experienced difficulties with scheduling, poor quality negatives, windy conditions, rain, light that was just too bright, missed appointments, car troubles, technical restrictions, among many others. Deborah Cruze wrote "…There never seems to be enough time and I always seemed to get 'there,' wherever 'there' is, and the light would be wrong, so however much time you think you need, you need about twice as much. As for fieldwork in Nye County, all the dust in Nevada ends up there."[3]

Within the arts, working collaboratively is not always easy, as each student discovers their individual and most independent method of working—day or night. Travel was difficult, distances were profound, and oftentimes the ranches were not what the students expected. While just about every student commented about the graciousness of the ranchers, there were those times, inevitably, when statements or actions were misunderstood. Photographers require time investigating a landscape, to walk around the barn, explore inside, time to find the right angle, the right light. The setup takes time, too, especially if they are work-

ing with large format 4x5 with the requisite tripod, bellows extension, dark cloth, and sheet film. The burden of the archive created expectations for performance, even if the scene is not ideal or the light faded. "Taking advantage of the opportunity" is such an appropriate phrase, declarative as well as directive. Unfortunately, the reality is something else. For example, Laura Fillmore regretted her inability to photograph the huge white owl that blew past her as she entered an historic barn in Dresslerville. It is always those photographs that were not made that humble us. If the students had more lecture presentations, more research, more time in the field, perhaps the archive could be two or three times as large.

After all is said and done, and as a consequence of these students' work, we have for future generations, for photography, for *history*, a profound record and archive of a transforming agricultural landscape in Nevada and within the Great Basin.[4] Although I am quite comfortable making this claim, perhaps it is for future generations to decide the worth of this archive, or for you.

Notes:
1. Email transmission from David Colburn dated Sunday, 17 March, 2002.
2. Email transmission from Deborah Cruze dated Monday, 24 June, 2002.
3. *Ibid.*
4. The archive, consisting of more than 420 photographs, is housed in the Special Collections Department, under the direction of Robert E. Blesse, Getchell Library, University of Nevada, Reno.

*The true basis for any serious study of the art of architecture is in those indigenous structures, the more humble buildings everywhere, which are to architecture what folklore is to literature or folksongs are to music . . . . All are happily content with what ornament and color they carry, as naturally as the rocks and trees and garden slopes which are with them.*

Frank Lloyd Wright, 1910

# Carson Valley: Where Nevada Began

The Carson Valley was first explored in 1833 and settled by Mormon farmers in 1851. They did not participate in the Valley's agricultural prosperity, resulting from the Comstock strike in 1859, because Brigham Young recalled them to Salt Lake. Henry Fred Dangberg settled in the Valley in the 1850s and within a short time he had created one of the major ranching operations in western Nevada. German settlers strongly influenced the culture and architecture of the Carson Valley. The boom years, 1860 to 1880, were followed by a period of quiet stability in which population remained steady. In recent decades population growth and suburban development have placed considerable pressure on ranch owners.

41

Ikue Yada. Interior, abandoned barn, corner of State Highway 206 and Limousine Court, Genoa.

Ikue Yada. Trimmer Barn, Genoa. Built in 1874 by Lorentz Frey, this barn was originally used to house racehorses for a racetrack located on the east edge of his property. When the property changed hands in 1909, the barn underwent a partial renovation. The north end of the barn was transformed into a milking parlor and a separator room was added.

Aimee Lopes.  Old metal saw, Williams Ranch, Genoa.

44

Jessica Slack. Hellwinkel Barn, Gardnerville. This barn was built in 1911. Half of the roof was replaced recently, thus half is metal and the other half wood shingles.

# Yerington: Ranch Culture in Mason Valley

In 1859, "Hock" Mason brought a herd of cattle to winter in a valley of the Walker River which now bears his name. His timing was perfect and he soon became one of the most successful livestock raisers in Nevada during the Comstock era.

Today, with approximately 50,000 acres under cultivation, Yerington is one of Nevada's leading agricultural areas. Local farmers grow alfalfa, onions, potatoes, and garlic, as well as specialized crops such as Jerusalem artichokes and wine grapes. Livestock operations include beef, sheep, dairy operations, llama breeding, and an ostrich farm.

Matt Thielen. Pump house in foreground, milk house in background, Capurro Ranch, Yerington.

47

Matt Thielen. Tack shed, Scatena Ranch, Yerington.

48

Matt Thielen. Cellar, Scierini Ranch, Yerington.

R. Nelson Parrish. Tack shed, built circa 1910, still in original use today, Scierini Ranch, Yerington.

# Reno, Sparks and Beyond:  Threatened Barns

For nearly a century, prosperous farms and ranches, fed by an intricate web of irrigation ditches, dominated life in the Truckee Meadows, home to Reno and Sparks. Italian farmers who emigrated to the Truckee Meadows during the late nineteenth and early twentieth centuries played an important role in northern Nevada agriculture. Today, however, little commercial agriculture takes place in the Truckee Meadows and only remnants of once handsome barns are left. Some Washoe County barns, such as the List Barn in Washoe Valley, have been restored for new uses.

51

Catana L. Barnes. Barn, Casazza Ranch, Reno.

Catana L. Barnes. Valley Road barn, Reno. Built circa 1870s.

Catana L. Barnes. Barn, Raffeto Ranch, Sparks. Built circa 1870-1880.

Deborah J. Cruze. Barn, List Ranch, Washoe Valley. Built circa 1934.

# Fallon: The Agricultural Heritage of the Newlands Project

Fallon, self-proclaimed "Oasis of Nevada," became an agricultural center because of the Reclamation Act of 1902, which was sponsored by Nevada Congressman Francis G. Newlands. This effort to make the desert bloom included the construction of two dams, Derby Dam on the Truckee River and Lahontan Dam on the Carson River, which provided the water necessary to develop agriculture in Fallon. In the last century, however, competition from northern Nevada's burgeoning population and the needs of the Pyramid Lake Paiute Tribe have placed pressure on this limited water supply.

Laura Fillmore. West elevation, two-stall horse barn, Kent Ranch, Stillwater. Built between 1970 and 1980.

Andrea Martinez. Corkill Ranch sign, Fallon.

Andrea Martinez. Gomes' water tower, Fallon.

Amber Lee Martin. Side view with fence, Kallenbach Barn, Fallon.

# Lovelock: Agriculture Along the Humboldt River

Originally founded as a railroad town, Lovelock is located in an area known as Big Meadow. The community turned to farming in the 1930s when the waters of the lower Humboldt River were impounded in the main channel to form Rye Patch Reservoir. Lovelock's main crops include alfalfa, seed, hay, wheat, barley, and oats.

Tsunaki Tabayashi. Barn, List Ranch, Lovelock.  Currently used as a garage and storage area.

Tsunaki Tabayashi. Barn, List Ranch, Lovelock.

Tsunaki Tabayashi. Barn, Moura Ranch, Lovelock.

64

Ryan Quinlan. Timber-frame barn, Arias Family Ranch, Lovelock.

# Paradise Valley:  Buckaroo Architecture in Far Northern Nevada

Mineral discoveries in Humboldt County led to the settlement of Paradise Valley. Mountains, including the 9,000 foot peaks of the Santa Rosa Range, ring Paradise Valley, which is about forty miles long and twelve miles wide. The ability of Paradise Valley ranchers to succeed in this harsh environment is due to the careful management of scarce water resources. Americans came; so did Germans, Basques, English, and Irish. Many families in Paradise Valley were from northern Italy and among them were skilled stonemasons. Adobe bricks from a local factory supplemented stone construction.

Deborah J. Cruze. Barn, Grayson Ranch, Paradise Valley.

Deborah J. Cruze. Barn, Bullhead Ranch, Humboldt County.

Deborah J. Cruze. Barn, Historic CD Bliss Ranch, Button Point.

Deborah J. Cruze. Adobe building with boxcar, Reeds Ranch, Paradise Valley.

# Eureka County:  Rural Architecture Along America's Loneliest Highway

A silver and lead boom in the 1870s put Eureka on the map. Small scale ranching and truck farming developed to supply the miners working in the district. During the mid-twentieth century various experimental crops were grown in Diamond Valley. These farmers finally settled on high quality alfalfa, which is sold to dairy operations in California or shipped to Japan in pellet form.

71

David W. Colborn. Barn, Melka Ranch, Eureka.  This structure served as a station for the Eureka-Palisades Railroad until about 1935—the first story was the depot and the second employee living quarters. Located about two miles north of Eureka.

David W. Colborn. Horse barn, side view, New Baumann Ranch, Eureka. This barn was built around 1960 with railroad ties from the defunct Eureka-Palisades Railroad. Located about three miles east of Eureka, this site is called "Hunters Ranch" on some maps.

David W. Colborn. Outbuilding #1, Old Baumann Ranch, Eureka. Located about 75 miles northeast of Eureka. Also known as the McClusky Ranch.

David W. Colborn. General view, Willow Creek Ranch.

# Nye County:  Ranching in the Mining Country of Central Nevada

As in many parts of Nevada, agriculture in Nye County was stimulated by the discovery of mining deposits, in this case in Ione in 1863 and Belmont in 1865. This is particularly true of Monitor Valley, which was settled by Jacob and Samuel Steininger in 1866. As the mines played out in central Nevada, some miners turned to ranching and agriculture. In the early years of the twentieth century, major strikes in Tonopah and Goldfield provided additional markets for Nye County ranchers.

Deborah J. Cruze. General view, Pine Creek Well.

Deborah J. Cruze. House, Pine Creek Well.

Deborah J. Cruze. Corral, Reed's Ranch.

Deborah J. Cruze. Barn, Moore's Station.

# Elko County:  The Ranches of Northeastern Nevada

Ranching in Elko County was established in the early 1850s to take advantage of emigrant wagon trains passing through the area. In 1859, Basque sheepherder Pedro Altube established the Spanish Ranch in the Elko region. Elko was only peripherally involved in the mining boom of the nineteenth century. Instead, ranchers in northeastern Nevada developed a thriving stock-raising industry. Rail transportation, which came to Elko in 1869, provided access to distant markets and thus insulated Elko County ranchers from the decline in mining after 1880. By the mid-1870s, for example, San Francisco acquired half of its beef from Nevada. However, severe weather and economic vicissitudes during the late 1880s led to the consolidation of ranches into large holdings. Today, ranching and gold mining are at the heart of the Elko County economy.

Anna Schooley. Modern shed with Zunino brand and equipment, Zunino Ranch, Jiggs.

David Brendan Torch. Barn, Keddy Ranch, north of Elko.

Ariana Page Russell. Ranch house, Zunino Ranch, Jiggs. Built in the early twentieth century and still in use.

Ariana Page Russell. Rear view of barn, Zaga Ranch, Jiggs.

# White Pine County: Ranching in the Copper Country of Eastern Nevada

Small-scale ranching operations were established in the nineteenth century to supply mining camps such as Eureka, Hamilton, Treasure City, and Eberhardt. The photographs included here show structures in the Duck Creek Basin built during the twentieth century copper boom. The waters of Duck Creek were diverted to the mining operations in McGill, and the mining companies owned most of the ranches in the basin in order to control this valuable resource.

Thomas Sanford Drew Boyer. Barn, north view, Bob Bell Ranch, Duck Creek Basin. Located about ten miles north of McGill.

87

Thomas Sanford Drew Boyer. Bunkhouse, looking west, Bob Bell Ranch.

Arlo Schenk. Barn, interior view looking west, Bob Bell Ranch.

89

Arlo Schenk. Barn, Pescio Saw Mill, Duck Creek Basin.

# Lincoln County:  Mormon Farming in Eastern Nevada

Miners in eastern Nevada "were silver seekers, eager to make quick fortunes and enjoy a luxurious life. . . . The Mormons, on the other hand, did not come to exploit the land, but to cultivate it. The Mormon settlers built stable, modest, comfortable homes and often supplemented their verdant fields with flowers. As a rule there were no bars or gambling rooms in the Mormon towns, and little of the hectic speculation which characterized the mining communities." James W. Hulse, *The Nevada Adventure*

Dustin Ray Hartman. Barn, Delmue Ranch, above Dry Valley, Lincoln County

92

Dustin Ray Hartman. Barn interior, East Panaca.

93

Dustin Ray Hartman. Barn interior, Delmue Ranch, above Dry Creek, Lincoln County

Nick Profaizer. Barn, Panaca.

# Logandale and Bunkerville: Architectural Remnants in Rural Clark County

Bunkerville on the Virgin River and Logandale on the Muddy River are both located in valleys north of where Lake Mead is today. Mormon farmers founded both communities. Members of the United Order, who were Mormons devoted to Utopianism, established Bunkerville in the 1870s. They successfully established a self-sufficient and communal settlement with processing mills for flour, cotton, and molasses, but dissention within the United Order led to the group's dissolution in the 1880s. For many decades Bunkerville was a community of independent farmers and dairymen. Today many community members work in casinos in nearby Mesquite.

Logandale, originally established by the Mormon Church in 1865, was abandoned for economic reasons in 1871. For nine years, non-Mormons took advantage of the property left behind. By 1880, Mormon settlers began to return to the area and eventually revitalized the communities of Overton, St. Thomas, and Logandale, formerly St. Joseph. With the coming of the railroad in the early years of the twentieth century, Logandale and surrounding communities developed a national market for their produce. The community shipped melons, radishes, and asparagus to consumers around North America. Logandale also produced the seeds of cotton and sugar beets, as well as tomato plants for large commercial producers. In the 1970s, competition from California growers and pressure for suburban development led to the rapid decline of agriculture in the community.

LaMont Johnson. Cistern, Bunkerville. This cistern was used to store water for livestock.

LaMont Johnson. Concrete and wood horse barn, Bunkerville.

LaMont Johnson. Living quarters, Huntsman Granary, Logandale. Adobe structure, built circa 1850s. This is a remnant of the long demolished Huntsman Granary that was located on the Solomon Huntsman Ranch.

99

LaMont Johnson. Farmhouse, Old Whitney Ranch, Bunkerville Mountains. This beautiful, isolated old ranch provides an oasis in these rugged red desert mountains. The Old Whitney Ranch supplied much of the fruit to the Moapa Valley and Bunkerville areas. Some of the original fruit trees remain.

# Timber-Frame Barns:  Nevada's Hidden Treasures

The ancient craft of timber framing was practiced in Nevada until the 1920s. Logs, most commonly formed into squared timbers, are cut on the ends to make an interlocking joint. Once the structural elements were created, the barn could be erected with community assistance at a one or two day "barn raising."

Deborah J. Cruze. Horse barn, Fulstone Ranch, Wellington. This now unusable barn was built circa 1850s.  It is currently scheduled for demolition and will be replaced with a modern barn designed to accommodate a riding camp for girls.

Jessica Slack. Hennigson Barn, Gardnerville.

Deborah J. Cruze. Barn door, Scossa Ranch, Genoa. Constructed in 1908 by Swiss craftsmen.

Ryan Quinlan. Rancher and timber-frame barn, historic Henry Van Sickle Station, Teig Family Ranch, Genoa. Barn built circa 1856.

# Timber-Frame Barns:  The Art of Joinery

Timber frame barns are held together with simple yet elegant mortise and tenon joints. Carefully crafted and secured with wooden pins, these joints can last for centuries. Scarf joints were used to join short timbers into a single, strong, piece.

Jessica Slack. Close up of joint, Hennigson Barn, Gardnerville. The barn was built circa 1890.

107

Jessica Slack. Hayloft showing joints, Hellwinkel Barn, Gardnerville. This barn was built in 1911. Half of the roof is new metal, half old wooden shingles.

Ryan Quinlan. Blade scarf joint with wedge, Burr Family Ranch, Minden.

109

Ryan Quinlan. Joint with pins, Burr Family Ranch, Minden.

# Building With Stone

A shortage of wood in many areas of Nevada led to the extensive
use of stone. Whether used in natural form or cut into blocks,
stone was used to construct barns and other ranch structures.

111

Thomas Sanford Drew Boyer. Crittenden Barn, Elko.

112

Andrea Martinez. Side view of large barn, Alpine Ranch, East of Fallon.

Deborah J. Cruze.  Smokehouse, 96 Ranch, Paradise Valley. Constructed of three materials: sandstone, volcanic rock, and adobe.

114

Deborah J. Cruze.  Ruin, Hot Creek Ranch, Nye County.

# The Stonemasons of Paradise Valley

In this secluded ranching district, stonemasons from the Italian Piedmont produced numerous stone structures starting in the 1860s and 1870s. Many of their designs, such as the bunkhouse on the Recanzone Ranch, reflect styles common in their north Italian homeland.

Deborah J. Cruze. Stone root cellar, HS Ranch, Paradise Valley. 1920 carved in concrete above door.

117

Deborah J. Cruze. Bunkhouse, Recanzone Ranch, Paradise Valley.  Built circa 1900.

Deborah J. Cruze. House, Bullhead Ranch, Humboldt County.

Deborah J. Cruze. Horse barn, 96 Ranch, Paradise Valley.  Built circa 1900.

# Willow Corrals and Sapling Fences: Adaptation to Scarcity

Unadorned and austere, the willow corrals and sapling fences of
Nevada ranches have an elegance and vigor associated with folk
design.

121

Deborah J. Cruze. Willow corral, 96 Ranch, Paradise Valley.

Jennifer Ober. Fence, Zaga Ranch, Jiggs.

123

Andrea Martinez. Fence from barn interior, Alpine Ranch, east of Fallon.

Ariana Page Russell. Shop, Gardner Ranch, Ruby Valley.  This structure
was built circa 1868, and constructed from bristlecone pine.

# Making Do: Railroad Tie Buildings

Railroad ties came into common use as a building material during the late nineteenth century. Owing to the haste with which the transcontinental railroad was constructed, the rights-of-way required improvement almost immediately, thus providing a new source of building materials. Other railroad ties became available as branch lines were abandoned or upgraded. Ranchers took advantage of this unexpected source of construction materials to build cabins, bunkhouses, and barns.

126

David Brendan Torch. Barn, Maggie Creek Ranch, Western Site, Northeastern Nevada.

David Brendan Torch. Barn detail, Maggie Creek Ranch, Western Site, Northeastern Nevada.

David W. Colborn. Horse barn, front view, New Baumann Ranch, Eureka.

Anna Schooley. Shed, McMullen Ranch, Jiggs.

# Metal Construction

Contemporary metal construction offers ranchers many advantages over traditional barn construction methods, such as lower initial cost and limited maintenance. Older metal sheds and outbuildings can also be seen on Nevada ranches and metal is often used to repair existing wood and stone structures.

131

Matt Theilen. Hog pen, Scatena Ranch, Yerington.

Ryan Quinlan. Replacement aluminum roof and wall, timber-frame barn, Burr Family Ranch, Minden.

133

Dustin Ray Hartman. Garage, Panaca.

134

David Brendan Torch. Shed, Keddy Ranch, north of Elko.

# Native American Ranch Structures

History of the Owyhee Horse Barn
From an interview with Shoshone Elder Earl Crum. Conducted by Laura Fillmore and Wes Barber, October 12, 2001, at the Crum residence in Owyhee.

*In 1936, my father was [a Bureau of Indian Affairs] policeman here. It's about that time when that barn was built. It was brand new at the time. The barn was mostly used by the Bureau of Indian Affairs employees. They kept their milk cows there, their horses. . . . Right next to the north and west side of the barn, there was a tribal bullpen. And the extension agent was in charge of that. Directly north of the barn there was a stock corral, made of heavy lumber. This is where they used to have their annual cattle sales.*

*My understanding is they brought those Hopis in from Arizona to do the rock mason work. They cut the stone by hand, and [the barn was] all made out of native stones. . . . Individual Indians had no use [for the barn], just the employees who might have [a] horse. One who had horses, I remember, was the chief of police. . . . But those policemen all had horses. They had the main use of it. As well as Matt Spenser [who] was the Indian agent. But Matt wasn't a bureaucrat; he was friend to all the Indians. (laughs)*

*And gradually—I don't know what year that barn was turned over to the tribe. And since they turned it over to the tribe, its more or less just became a way house, which it is now. It's not used . . . [as] a horse barn or cow barn. . . .*

*. . . So that's the history of that barn. But like I said, there was corrals around there, and the Indians worked near there when they were building the fence, I remember, about 1936, they used the corrals to stockpile their fence posts. At that time, they were rebuilding the fence around the reservation, and they employed many Indians from the reservation. Even I worked on there, when I worked for the CCC [Civilian Conservation Corps].*

Laura Fillmore. Shoshone barn, southeast view, Owyhee.  Hopi stonemasons built this barn for the Indian agency in 1931.

137

Laura Fillmore.  South elevation, Washoe horse barn in foreground, cow barn in background, Dresslerville.

Laura Fillmore.  Portrait of Daniel McDonald, Steven James, and Steven's grandson Jimmie Bryan, Dresslerville.

Deborah J. Cruze. Ruins, Peavine Canyon, Nye County.

# Ranch Houses

The ranch house is the heart of a ranching operation. It is home, office, and "command central." Ranch houses tend to represent a length of occupation unheard of in suburbia. Often, generations of ranching families have lived and worked within. Nevada ranch houses reflect a mix of function and style denoting their period of construction—executed to vernacular standards. Late nineteenth and early twentieth century ranch houses may sport Victorian massing and decorative gingerbread. A little later, the Craftsman bungalow style left its mark. Regardless of its physical manifestation, the ranch house is the hub of a working ranch.

141

David Brendan Torch. Cabins, PX Ranch, north of Elko.

Deborah J. Cruze. Spanish Ranch, Tuscarora.

Deborah J. Cruze. 96 Ranch, Paradise Valley. Built circa 1895.

144

Matt Theilen. Capurro Ranch, Yerington.

# The Privy

Rural outhouses have endured longer than their urban counterparts, which went the way of comfort and decorum with the first municipal sanitation systems. Serving a universal function, the remains of Nevada privies can be found alongside ranch houses and bunkhouses, and at remote grazing camps. Ranch pit privies were often located close to wells and other domestic water sources or suspended over irrigation ditches, which led the federal government to take an interest in rural sanitary conditions in 1938, when the Works Progress Administration (WPA), in conjunction with the State Board of Health, sponsored the Nevada Fly-proof Privy Program. For a small fee to each property owner, WPA workers constructed state-of-the art, concrete-lined privies on ranches throughout the state. Nearly 1,100 WPA privies were built in rural Nevada.

Dustin Ray Hartman. Spring Mountain Ranch, near Red Rock.

Deborah J. Cruze. Barn with outhouse, San Antonio Ranch, Nye County.

David Brendan Torch. WPA privy, Keddy Ranch, north of Elko.

149

David Brendan Torch. Upper Tule Ranch, north of Elko.

# Rural Cathedrals

Standing in a large and historic barn has much in common with being inside a great cathedral. The vastness and volume of the space, coupled with the quality of light, elicit a sublime sense of wonder. The aroma of hay and cattle is the incense that completes the experience.

151

Thomas Sanford Drew Boyer. Six Bar Ranch, Elko.

152

Jessica Slack. Hennigson Barn, Gardnerville.

Jessica Slack. White Barn, Gardnerville.

154

Jessica Slack. Hellwinkel Barn, Gardnerville.

# Barn Interiors

Over the years, old barns have performed many functions, from husbandry to workshop, and all of these operations leave their debris behind. Barns are also used for the storage of miscellaneous and unrelated household, recreational, and ranch goods. This kaleidoscope of stuff creates a crazy quilt where anvils, tack, wheel chairs, and Halloween decorations may reside in harmony for decades.

Jennifer Ober. Working barn with old tack, Gardner Ranch, Ruby Valley.

157

Matt Theilen. Bunkhouse, Capurro Ranch, Yerington.

Matt Theilen. Milk house, Capurro Ranch, Yerington.

159

Matt Theilen. Cattle shed, Capurro Ranch, Yerington.

# Gambrel Roofs

"A roof having two flat surfaces on each side of a central ridge; each surface is at a different pitch; the shorter upper surface has a low pitch, and the longer, lower surface, has a steep pitch. A gambrel roof is more complicated to build than a gable roof, but it provides greater headroom under the roof than does a pitched roof covering the same floor area, hence its wide use in barn construction." (Cyril M. Harris, *American Architecture: An Illustrated Encyclopedia*, N.Y., 1998, p. 144.)

The gambrel roof gets its name from its similarity in shape to the somewhat crooked hind leg of a horse. The term gambrel is also used to describe the comparably shaped bent stick used to hang an animal carcass during dressing.

161

Laura Fillmore. North Elevation, Shoshone Barn, Owyhee. Built in 1931 by Hopi stonemasons.

Dustin Ray Hartman. Barn, Delmue Ranch, above Dry Valley, Lincoln County.

163

David Brendan Torch. Barn, PX Ranch, north of Elko.

Ariana Page Russell. Smith Brothers OX Ranch, Ruby Valley.

# Gable and Basilica Roofs and Cupolas

Barns in Nevada most commonly have simple gable roofs. There are many variations on this design including the use of air vents or cupolas. Another adaptation is the basilica roof, which is named after the public hall that formed a gathering point in every Roman city. The basilica style became the inspiration for early Christian churches. A clerestory characterizes the basilica design; a wall, most commonly with windows, rises at the point where the central bay and the side aisles meet, creating a roof on two planes.

LaMont Johnson. Old Capalappa Ranch Barn, Logandale.

167

Amber Lee Martin. Kallenbach Barn, basilica or clerestory roof, Fallon.

168

Jessica Slack. White Barn, Gardnerville.

Tsunaki Tabayashi. Arias Ranch, Lovelock.

# Gable Roof Barns With Wings

Barns with a simple gable roof and sheds or wings on either side
are the essence of the Nevada barn style. This straightforward yet
graceful design reflects much about life on a Nevada ranch.

171

Deborah J. Cruze. Old Cerri Ranch, Paradise Valley.

Nick Profaizer. Hayloft and tool shed, Eagle Valley Barn, Lincoln County.

173

Catana L. Barnes. Quilici Barn, Reno. Built between 1900 and 1910.

Ikue Yada. Trimmer Barn, Genoa. Built in 1874.

# Other Rural Buildings

Ranch houses and barns are the most prominent buildings on a Nevada ranch. However, other structures, particularly in the past, were common elements on a working spread. These might include a sawmill, blacksmith shop, tool shed, tack shed, potato or root cellar, milk house, granary, water tower, line cabin, creamery, chicken coop, tanning shed, and smokehouse.

Andrea Martinez. Water tower, Seven Hanging Hearts Ranch, Fallon.

David W. Colborn. Root cellar, New Baumann Ranch, Eureka. Built from logs and railroad ties.

178

Deborah J. Cruze. House converted into a church, San Antonio Ranch, Nye County.

LaMont Johnson. Concrete silo, Bunkerville.

179

# Barns and Basketball

The basketball hoops found on many Nevada barns remind us that ranches are often homes for families—families with children—not simply factories for the production of beef.

Aimee Lopes. Barn, Hanson Ranch, Carson Valley.

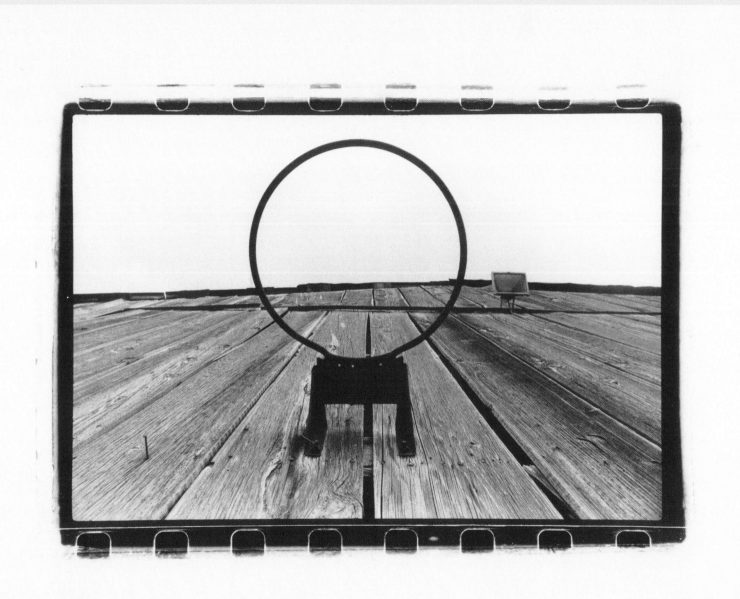

182

Nick Profaizer. Barn, Lincoln County.

183

Anna Schooley. Barnes Ranch, Spring Creek.

184

Matt Theilen. Blacksmith shop, Scierini Ranch, Yerington.

# Ranch Portraits: People and Place

People and their intimate relationship with place are central to the experience of family ranching in Nevada. In these four portraits, rural Nevadans are juxtaposed with ranch structures, revealing something of the strength of the people and the land.

David W. Colborn. Ranch Hand John Wilker with Rowdy in front of horse barn, Walti Ranch, Eureka.

187

David Brendan Torch. Susan Church in her barn workshop, Keddy Ranch, north of Elko.

LaMont Johnson. Lawrence Marshall beside outhouse, Logandale.

189

Laura Fillmore. Earl Crum, Owyhee